Investigate Math

Grade 3

by Cindi Mitchell

Editor: Maria L. Chang
Cover design: Cynthia Ng
Interior design: Grafica, Inc.
Cover images © Shutterstock.com.
Interior art: Mike Moran (4); Noun Project (all remaining art)

ISBN: 978-1-338-75170-3
Scholastic Inc., 557 Broadway, New York, NY 10012

Table of Contents

Introduction

Welcome to *Investigate Math*! This book offers dozens of engaging activities designed to give students multiple opportunities to deeply investigate math concepts. Instead of memorizing algorithms and facts to solve a math problem, students need to look at the problem from various angles and see how new concepts fit into what they already know about mathematics. They need to apply their learning in different ways, brainstorm how to solve problems, shift to a new strategy when the current one is not working, and understand abstract concepts. In other words, they need to develop flexible thinking skills.

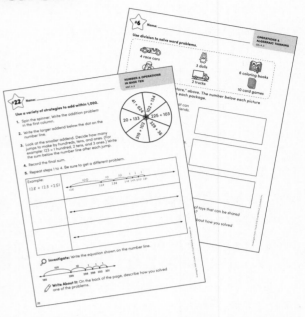

In its 2012 global survey, the Programme for International Student Assessment (PISA) found that in every country students who memorized mathematical concepts were the lowest achievers. Students who use relational strategies and self-monitoring may initially struggle to work through mathematical concepts, but once they thoroughly understand a concept, they build a strong foundation that allows them to file and catalog the information so they can recall and apply it later. Our goal in developing this book is to help students build a strong foundational framework in mathematics that they can readily access and apply to various real-life situations.

How to Use This Book

Students can work on the activities in this book independently, with a partner, or in small groups. The activities build on concepts and skills that you have already taught, but they offer opportunities to expand students' understanding in various ways—from investigating through the use of manipulatives to exploring through representational drawings. What makes the problems in this book unique is that there is no one correct answer for most of them. This allows students to make and share a variety of math problems and solutions using the same activity page. Encourage students to describe their answers using mathematical language—an important part of today's rigorous standards that is often overlooked in math instruction.

Some activities require the use of a spinner, which is printed on the page. To use the spinner, have students place a paper clip on the spinner and use a pencil to hold one end of the clip in place at the center of the spinner. Then, flick a finger to make the paper clip spin.

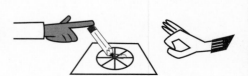

Each activity comes with an Investigate section, which challenges advanced learners to solve difficult problems or to investigate new concepts at a higher level. Also on every page is a section entitled Write About It (see below). Through writing, students boost long-term memory as they begin to see patterns and better understand how the new concepts relate to their overall understanding of mathematics. After students have completed the writing activity, invite them to share and discuss their responses with a classmate. This provides another essential way for students to reflect on what they have learned, to refine their thinking, and to make connections.

Formative Assessments Ideas

Formative assessments are a great way to evaluate students' strengths and weaknesses. Here are some quick and easy formative assessment ideas.

Write About It: In the Write About It section on each page, students reflect on what they have learned in the activity. For example, students may write the definition of a term in their own words, describe the steps taken to solve a problem, or describe one of the most important concepts learned from the lesson. These written responses help students synthesize what they learned and often provide a quick way to gauge their understanding.

Self-Assessment: After students finish a lesson, ask them to describe their level of understanding of the topic by writing a single word, phrase, or emoji at the top of the page, followed by a one-sentence explanation. For example: "Got It," "Still Trying," "Need Help," or "☺," "☹." Using this technique will not only help you evaluate student comprehension, but it also provides students with an opportunity to reflect and assess their own understanding.

Pair and Share: Provide a conversation prompt and pair up students to discuss. This can provide you with another assessment tool as you circulate around the room listening to conversations. Here are a few prompts to get started:

What is one important idea you want to remember from this lesson? Why do you think it is important?

What was the most difficult part of this lesson and why?

What is one question you have about the lesson today?

As students work through the activities in this book, encourage them to investigate deeply, ask hard questions, and share what they are learning. We hope that they will discover that mathematics is so much more than memorizing algorithms and getting right answers. It is in fact about curiosity, investigation, making connections, and having loads of fun!

Math Standards Correlations

The activities in this book meet the following core standards in mathematics.

OPERATIONS & ALGEBRAIC THINKING
OA.A.1 Interpret products of whole numbers, e.g., interpret 5 × 7 as the total number of objects in 5 groups of 7 objects each.
OA.A.2 Interpret whole-number quotients of whole numbers, e.g., interpret 56 ÷ 8 as the number of objects in each share when 56 objects are partitioned equally into 8 shares, or as a number of shares when 56 objects are partitioned into equal shares of 8 objects each.
OA.A.3 Use multiplication and division within 100 to solve word problems in situations involving equal groups, arrays, and measurement quantities.
OA.A.4 Determine the unknown whole number in a multiplication or division equation relating three whole numbers.
OA.B.5 Apply properties of operations as strategies to multiply and divide. (Commutative property of multiplication, associative property of multiplication, distributive property)
OA.B.6 Understand division as an unknown-factor problem.
OA.C.7 Fluently multiply and divide within 100, using strategies such as the relationship between multiplication and division or properties of operations.
OA.D.8 Solve two-step word problems using the four operations.
OA.D.9 Identify arithmetic patterns (including patterns in the addition table or multiplication table) and explain them using properties of operations.
NUMBER & OPERATIONS IN BASE TEN
NBT.A.1 Use place value understanding to round whole numbers to the nearest 10 or 100.
NBT.A.2 Fluently add and subtract within 1,000 using strategies and algorithms based on place value, properties of operations, and/or the relationship between addition and subtraction.
NBT.A.3 Multiply one-digit whole numbers by multiples of 10 in the range 10–90.
NUMBER & OPERATIONS: FRACTIONS
NF.A.1 Understand a fraction 1/b as the quantity formed by 1 part when a whole is partitioned into b equal parts; understand a fraction a/b as the quantity formed by a parts of size 1/b.
NF.A.2 Understand a fraction as a number on the number line; represent fractions on a number line diagram.
NF.A.3 Explain equivalence of fractions in special cases and compare fractions by reasoning about their size.
MEASUREMENT & DATA
MD.A.1 Tell and write time to the nearest minute and measure time intervals in minutes. Solve word problems involving addition and subtraction of time intervals in minutes, e.g., by representing the problem on a number line diagram.
MD.A.2 Measure and estimate liquid volumes and masses of objects using standard units of grams (g), kilograms (kg), and liters (l).
MD.B.3 Draw a scaled picture graph and a scaled bar graph to represent a data set with several categories.
MD.B.4 Generate measurement data by measuring lengths using rulers marked with halves and fourths of an inch. Show the data by making a line plot.
MD.C.5 Recognize area as an attribute of plane figures and understand concepts of area measurement.
MD.C.6 Measure areas by counting unit squares.
MD.C.7 Relate area to the operations of multiplication and addition.
MD.D.8 Solve real world and mathematical problems involving perimeters of polygons.
GEOMETRY
G.A.1 Understand that shapes in different categories may share attributes and that the shared attributes can define a larger category. Recognize rhombuses, rectangles, and squares as examples of quadrilaterals and draw examples of quadrilaterals that do not belong to any of these subcategories.
G.A.2 Partition shapes into parts with equal areas. Express the area of each part as a unit fraction of the whole.

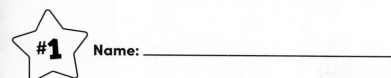

#1 Name: _____

Use groupings of objects to interpret products of whole numbers.

⊘ **You will need:** number cube

1. Roll the number cube until you get a number greater than 1. Draw that many large circles in the box below.

2. Roll the number cube again until you get a different number greater than 1. Draw that many squares inside each circle.

3. How many squares do you have in all? _____

4. Write a multiplication sentence to show your work.

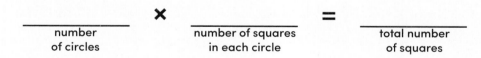

| _____ | **✗** | _____ | **=** | _____ |
| number of circles | | number of squares in each circle | | total number of squares |

5. What would happen if you swapped the number of circles and the number of squares in the problem above? Write a multiplication sentence. Create a drawing on the back of the page.

_____ **✗** _____ **=** _____

🔍 **Investigate:** Did the order of the factors change the product? Did the order of the factors change the drawing? Explain.

✏️ **Write About It:** On the back of the page, define the term *multiplication* in your own words.

#**2** Name: _____

Use arrays to interpret products of whole numbers.

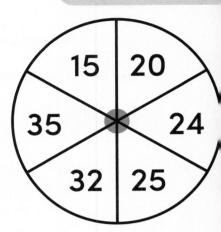

⊘ **You will need:** counters

1. Spin the spinner. Write the target number. _____

2. Grab that number of counters. Use the counters to make an array on your desk. Draw a picture of your array.

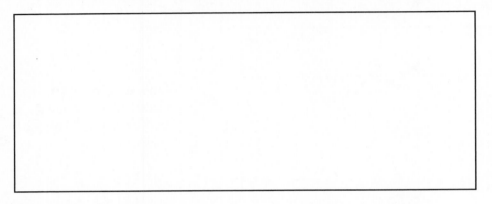

> An **array** is a model that shows objects in rows and columns. We can use arrays to help solve multiplication problems.
>
>
>
> 2 rows of 3 objects:
> $2 \times 3 = 6$

3. Write a multiplication sentence that matches your array.

_____

🔍 **Investigate:** How many different arrays can you make using the counters? Draw pictures of your arrays. Write a multiplication sentence for each array.

 Write About It: On the back of the page, define the term *array* in your own words.

#3 Name: _____

Interpret whole-number quotients of whole numbers.

✓ **You will need:** counters • paper

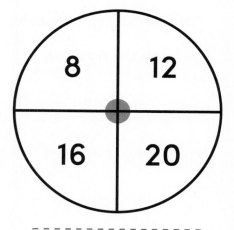

The spinner shows: 8, 12, 16, 20

1. Spin the spinner. Write the target number in the box.

[ ] ÷ 4 = _____

Grab that number of counters. Draw four squares on a sheet of paper. Place one counter at a time in each square until you've used up all of the counters. Draw a picture of your work.

[ ] [ ] [ ] [ ]

How many counters are in each box? _____
Complete the division problem above.

> One way we can think about division is to find how many objects are in each group.
>
>
>
> There are 4 hearts in each group: 12 ÷ 3 = 4

2. Spin the spinner again. Write the target number in the box.

[ ] ÷ 2 = _____

Grab that number of counters. Draw two squares on a sheet of paper. Place one counter at a time in each square until you've used up all of the counters. Draw a picture of your work.

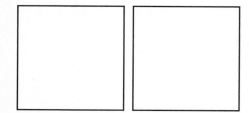

How many counters are in each box? _____
Complete the division problem above.

🔍 **Investigate:** Find the unknown number. Then, describe how you solved the problem.   _____ ÷ 2 = 5

✏️ **Write About It:** On the back of the page, define the term *division* in your own words.

Interpret whole-number quotients of whole numbers.

1. Spin the spinner. Count the hearts.
   Write the number in the box.

   [ ] ÷ **3** = _____

   Draw a picture of the hearts below.
   Circle groups of 3 hearts.

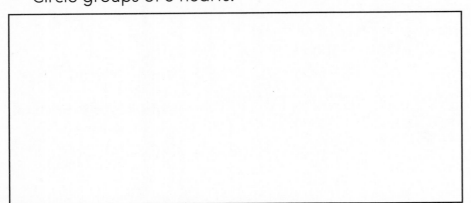

   How many groups do you have? _____
   Complete the division sentence above.

2. Repeat step 1.
   Spin the spinner until you get
   a different number of hearts.

   [ ] ÷ **3** = _____

   How many groups do you have? _____
   Complete the division sentence above.

One way we can think about division is to find the number of equal groups.

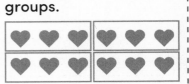

We have 4 groups of 3 hearts.

12 ÷ 4 = 3

🔍 **Investigate:** Write and solve a division problem. Label the divisor, dividend, and quotient.

 Write About It: On the back of the page, write a division word problem. Explain how to solve it.

#5 Name: _____

Use multiplication to solve word problems.

✓ **You will need:** number cube

Diana has a vegetable garden with rows of carrots, radishes, and onions.
She planted each vegetable in 4 rows.

1. Roll the number cube. This is the number of vegetables Diana planted in each of the 4 rows. If you roll 1, try again.

   Carrots _____   Radishes _____   Onions _____

2. Create an array or draw a picture to show the total number of each vegetable.

Carrots	Write the multiplication equation.
	_____
	How many carrots in all? _____

Radishes	Write the multiplication equation.
	_____
	How many radishes in all? _____

Onions	Write the multiplication equation.
	_____
	How many onions in all? _____

🔍 **Investigate:** Say Diana planted only 3 rows of each vegetable. How many carrots, radishes, and onions would she have?

✏️ **Write About It:** On the back of the page, explain how you solved one of the problems.

Use division to solve word problems.

4 race cars

3 dolls

6 coloring books

12 marbles

2 trucks

10 card games

Look at the toys in the "toy store," above. The number below each picture shows the number of items in each package.

1. Choose a package of toys that can be shared equally among 3 friends. Draw a picture.

Write the division equation.

_____

2. Choose a package of toys that can be shared equally between 2 friends. Draw a picture.

Write the division equation.

_____

3. Choose a package of toys that can be shared equally among 5 friends. Draw a picture.

Write the division equation.

_____

🔍 **Investigate:** Is there more than one package of toys that can be shared equally between 2 people? If so, which ones?

✏️ **Write About It:** On the back of the page, write about how you solved one of the word problems.

#7 Name: _____

Determine the unknown whole number in a multiplication equation.

We can use an array to find the unknown factor in a multiplication equation.

$$? \times 5 = 15$$

? = number of rows × 5 = objects in each row = 15 = total number of objects

} 3 rows

$$3 \times 5 = 15$$

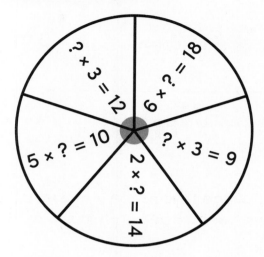

1. Spin the spinner. Write the multiplication equation.

   _____

   Draw an array to find the unknown factor.

   What is the unknown factor? _____

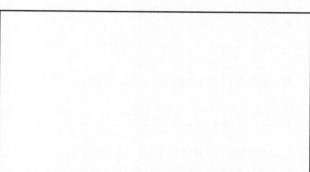

2. Spin the spinner to get a different equation. Write the equation.

   _____

   Draw an array to find the unknown factor.

   What is the unknown factor? _____

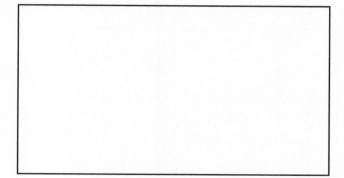

 Investigate: Write a multiplication equation with an unknown whole number. Be sure to include the answer.

 Write About It: Say a friend asked you, "How do I find an unknown factor in a multiplication equation?" On the back of the page, write what you would say. Use the terms *factor* and *product*.

Determine the unknown whole number in a division equation.

1. Spin the spinner.
    Write the division equation.

    _____

    Draw a picture to find the unknown number.

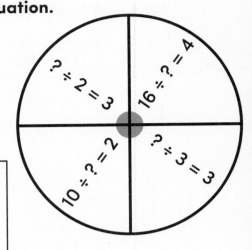

    What is the unknown number? _____

2. Spin the spinner to get a different equation.
    Write the division equation.

    _____

    Draw a picture to find the unknown number.

    What is the unknown number? _____

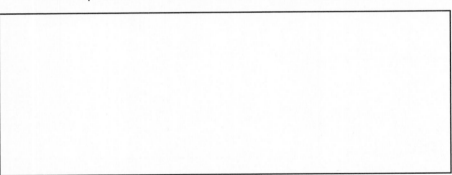

    Investigate: Say you have 12 cards. You want to place them in rows.
    Each row has the same number. How many ways can you arrange the cards?

    Write About It: On the back of the page, write about the most important
    idea you learned in this lesson.

Understand and apply the Commutative Property of Multiplication.

Commutative Property of Multiplication: If you change the order of the factors, the product will stay the same.

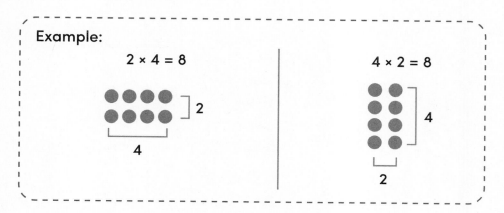

Example:

$2 \times 4 = 8$

$4 \times 2 = 8$

1. Write two multiplication sentences that show the Commutative Property of Multiplication.

    _____ × _____ = _____   _____ × _____ = _____

2. Model the Commutative Property of Multiplication. Draw an array to show each multiplication sentence above.

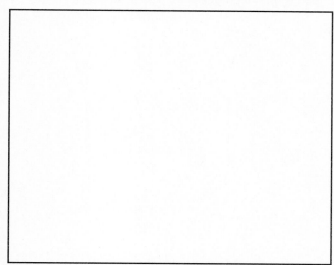

Investigate: Describe the two arrays above. How are they the same? How are they different?

Write About It: In your own words, write about the Commutative Property of Multiplication. What does the rule say? How can you apply it?

#10 Name: _____

Understand and apply the Associative Property of Multiplication.

Associative Property of Multiplication: If you change the way the factors are grouped, the product will stay the same.

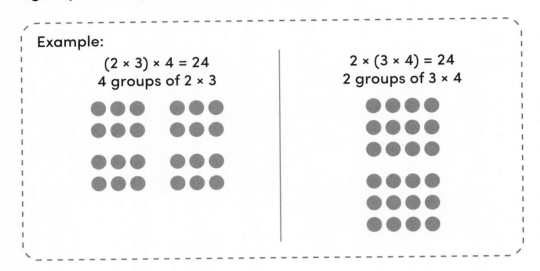

Example:

$(2 × 3) × 4 = 24$
4 groups of 2 × 3

$2 × (3 × 4) = 24$
2 groups of 3 × 4

1. Write two multiplication sentences that show the Associative Property of Multiplication.

    (_____ × _____) × _____ = _____

    _____ × (_____ × _____) = _____

2. Model the Associative Property of Multiplication. Draw an array to show each multiplication sentence above.

🔍 **Investigate:** Describe the two arrays above. How are they the same? How are they different?

✏️ **Write About It:** In your own words, write about the Associative Property of Multiplication. What does the rule say? How can you apply it?

Understand and apply the Distributive Property of Multiplication.

The Distributive Property of Multiplication: Say you multiply the sum of two addends by a number. If you multiply each addend by the number and then add the products together, you will get the same result.

1. Write a multiplication sentence that shows the Distributive Property of Multiplication.

   ____ × (____ + ____) = (____ × ____) + (____ × ____)

2. Use the Distributive Property to solve this multiplication problem: **5 × 8 = n.**

   Draw a line to show one way to break up the array. Then, fill in the missing information.

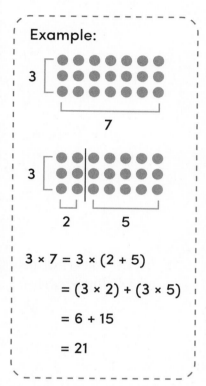

Example:

$3 \times 7 = 3 \times (2 + 5)$

$= (3 \times 2) + (3 \times 5)$

$= 6 + 15$

$= 21$

5 [array] 8

$5 \times 8 = 5 \times (\underline{} + \underline{})$

$= (5 \times \underline{}) + (5 \times \underline{})$

$= \underline{} + \underline{}$

$= \underline{}$

 Investigate: Show another way to break up the array. Then, fill in the missing information.

5 [array] 8

$5 \times 8 = 5 \times (\underline{} + \underline{})$

$= (5 \times \underline{}) + (5 \times \underline{})$

$= \underline{} + \underline{}$

$= \underline{}$

✏️ **Write About It:** On the back of the page, write about the Distributive Property of Multiplication in your own words. What does the rule say? How can you apply it?

17

#12 Name: _____

Understand division as an unknown-factor problem.

$7 \times 8 = 56$ $6 \times 9 = 54$ $6 \times 3 = 18$ $5 \times 5 = 25$

$9 \times 3 = 27$ $8 \times 4 = 32$ $7 \times 3 = 21$ $7 \times 6 = 42$

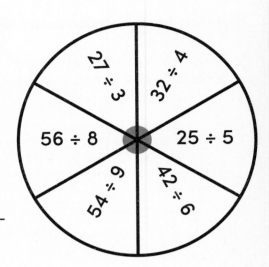

1. Spin the spinner.
   Write the division sentence. _____

   Which of the multiplication
   sentences above can help
   you solve the problem? _____

   Write the quotient. _____

2. Spin the spinner to get a
   different division sentence.
   Write the division problem. _____

   Which of the multiplication
   sentences above can help
   you solve the problem? _____

   Write the quotient. _____

Multiplication and division are related. They are known as inverse, or opposite, operations.

$2 \times 3 = 6$

$6 \div 3 = 2$

 Investigate: Write your
own division sentence. _____

Write a multiplication
sentence that can help
you solve the problem. _____

Write the quotient. _____

 Write About It: Why do you think multiplication and division are called
"inverse, or opposite, operations"?

#13 Name: _____

Understand division as an unknown-factor problem.

1. Spin the spinner. Write the number combination. _____

   Use the three numbers to write a division sentence. _____

   Draw an array to model the division sentence.

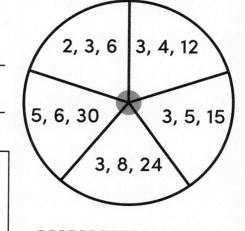

   Use the same three numbers to write a multiplication sentence. _____

2. Spin the spinner to get a different number combination. Write the number combination. _____

   Use the three numbers to write a division sentence. _____

   Draw an array to model the division sentence.

   Use the same three numbers to write a multiplication sentence. _____

We can use arrays to show division and multiplication.

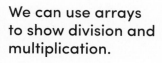

12 ÷ 2 = 6
number in all / number of rows / number in each row

2 × 6 = 12
number of rows / number in each row / number in all

 Investigate: Can you use the same three numbers in one division sentence to create a different division sentence? Explain.

 Write About It: On the back of the page, describe how multiplication and division are the same and different.

#14 **Name:** _____

Multiply within 100.

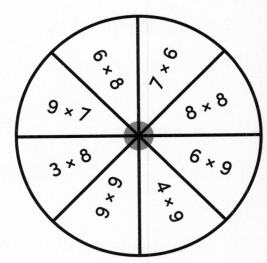

1. Spin the spinner.

2. Pick a strategy to solve the problem: array, repeated addition, or draw a picture.

3. Write the multiplication problem in the correct column below. Find the product using the strategy you chose. Show your work.

4. Repeat steps 1 to 3 to complete the chart. Be sure to get a different multiplication problem each time. Use a different strategy for each problem.

Array	Repeated Addition	Draw a Picture

Investigate: Write three different multiplication sentences that have a product of 20.

_____ _____ _____

Write About It: On the back of the page, write which strategy you like best for finding products. Explain why.

#15 Name: _____

Divide within 100.

1. Spin the spinner.

2. Pick a strategy to solve the problem: array, repeated subtraction, or draw a picture.

3. Write the division problem in the correct column below. Find the quotient using the strategy you chose. Show your work.

4. Repeat steps 1 to 3 to complete the chart. Be sure to get a different division problem each time. Use a different strategy for each problem.

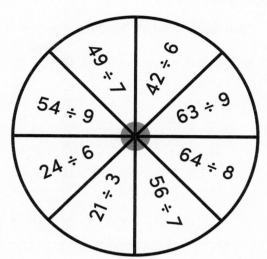

Array	Repeated Subtraction	Draw a Picture

Investigate: Write three different division sentences that have a quotient of 4.

_____ _____ _____

Write About It: On the back of the page, write which strategy you like best for finding quotients. Explain why.

★ **#16** **Name:** _____

Solve two-step word problems using the four operations.

Spin the spinner to fill in the missing numbers.

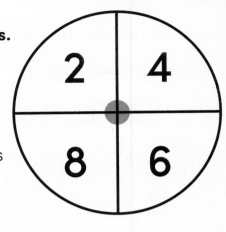

1. Paul has _____ packs of baseball cards. Each
pack has _____ cards. His friend Omar has
_____ packs of baseball cards with _____ cards
in each pack. The boys want to collect 150 cards
altogether. How many more cards do they need?
Use objects or drawings to help solve the problem.

Solution: _____

2. Lily collected eggs 7 days in a row. Each day she collected _____
eggs. On the eighth day, she ate the eggs she had collected over
2 days. How many eggs does Lily have left from the week?
Use a tape diagram or other drawing to help solve the problem.

Solution: _____

🔍 **Investigate:** On the back of the page, describe the process you used
to solve word problems. Did you use a step-by-step plan?

✏️ **Write About It:** On the back of the page, write a word problem that
uses two operations. Be sure to include the answer.

Solve two-step word problems using the four operations.

Spin the spinner to fill in the missing numbers.

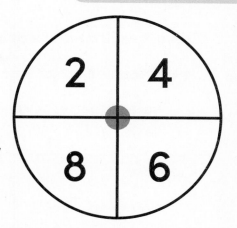

1. Francesca has a postcard book. Each page holds 2 postcards. She already has _____ pages filled. Now, Francesca got _____ new postcards. When she puts the new postcards in the book, how many pages will be filled in all? Use objects or drawings to help solve the problem. Write an equation. Use a letter for the unknown amount.

Equation: _____ Solution: _____

2. The students in Mr. Brown's class are recording how many boxes of donuts they sell. Their goal is to sell at least 100 boxes. If _____ students sell _____ boxes, how many more boxes do they need to sell? Use objects or drawings to help solve the problem. Write an equation. Use a letter for the unknown amount.

Equation: _____ Solution: _____

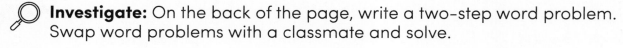

Investigate: On the back of the page, write a two-step word problem. Swap word problems with a classmate and solve.

Write About It: On the back of the page, write about one strategy you used to make sure that your answers to word problems are reasonable.

#18 Name: _____

Identify arithmetic patterns in the addition table.

✓ **You will need:** Addition Table (page 61) • crayons

1. Shade the row and column blue for the addend 0. Write three number sentences that show the sum of an addend and 0.

What do you notice about the sum of any addend and 0?

_____

2. Show two different ways of writing 7 as the sum of 3 and 4.

What do you notice about the sum of addends when the order is changed?

_____

 Investigate: Look at the Addition Table. Find examples of the addends described below. Complete each sentence.

The sum of two even addends is always _____.

The sum of an even addend and an odd addend is always _____.

The sum of two odd addends is always _____.

 Write About It: What is one of the most important ideas you learned from this lesson? Write about it on the back of the page.

Identify arithmetic patterns in the Multiplication Table.

✓ **You will need:** Multiplication Table (page 62) • crayons

1. Shade the row and column red for the factor 1. Write three number sentences that show the product of a factor and 1.

What do you notice about the product of any factor and 1?

_____

2. Show two different ways of writing 12 as the product of 3 and 4.

What do you notice about the product of factors when the order is changed?

_____

 Investigate: Look at the Multiplication Table. Find examples of the factors described below. Complete each sentence.

The product of two even factors is always _____.

The product of an even factor and an odd factor is always _____.

The product of two odd factors is always _____.

 Write About It: What is one of the questions that you had during this lesson? Did you find the answer? Write about it on the back of the page.

#20 Name: _____

Round numbers to the nearest 10.

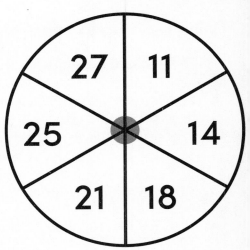

✓ **You will need:** base ten blocks

1. Spin the spinner. Write the number in the chart.

2. On your desk, model the number using base ten blocks. Then, draw a picture below.

3. Identify your benchmark numbers.

4. Round the number to the nearest ten.

5. Repeat steps 1 to 4. Be sure to get a different number.

Example: 16	Write the number: _____	Write the number: _____
10 16 20 benchmark numbers		
Rounds to __20__	Rounds to _____	Rounds to _____

🔍 **Investigate:** Choose any two-digit number. Round that number to the nearest ten. Can you find another two-digit number that rounds to the same number?

✏️ **Write About It:** On the back of the page, define the term *round* in your own words.

#21 Name: _____

Round numbers to the nearest 100.

✓ **You will need:** base ten blocks

1. Spin the spinner. Write the number in the chart.

2. On your desk, model the number using base ten blocks. Then, draw a picture below.

3. Identify your benchmark numbers.

4. Round the number to the nearest hundred.

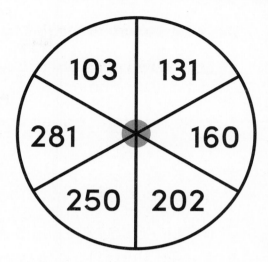

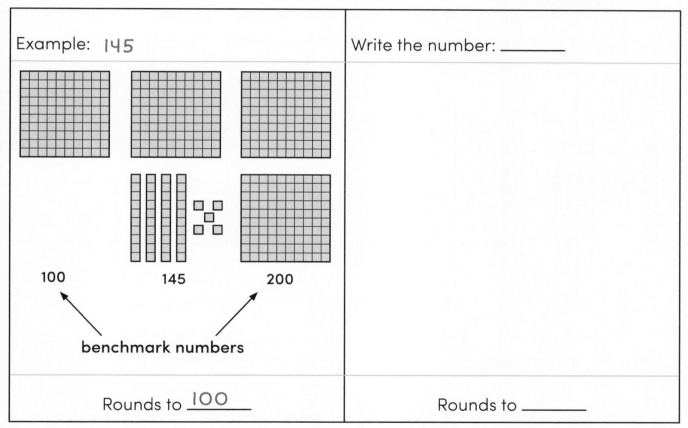

Example: 145

100   145   200

benchmark numbers

Rounds to __100__

Write the number: _____

Rounds to _____

🔍 **Investigate:** Choose any three-digit number. Round the number to the nearest hundred. Can you find another three-digit number that rounds to the same number?

✏️ **Write About It:** On the back of the page, describe the steps you took to solve the problem.

#22 **Name:** _____

NUMBER & OPERATIONS
IN BASE TEN
NBT.A.2

Use a variety of strategies to add within 1,000.

1. Spin the spinner. Write the addition problem in the first column.

2. Write the larger addend below the dot on the number line.

3. Look at the smaller addend. Decide how many jumps to make by hundreds, tens, and ones. (For example: 123 = 1 hundred, 2 tens, and 3 ones.) Write the sum below the number line after each jump.

4. Record the final sum.

5. Repeat steps 1 to 4. Be sure to get a different problem.

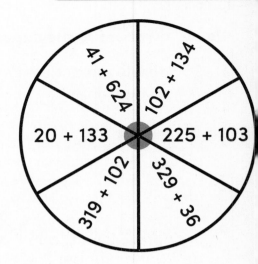

Example:	
128 + 123 = 251	100 10 10 1 1 1 128 228 238 248 249 250 251

Investigate: Write the equation shown on the number line.

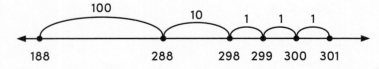

100   10   1   1   1

188   288   298 299 300 301

Write About It: On the back of the page, describe how you solved one of the problems.

28

#23 Name: _____

Use a variety of strategies to subtract within 1,000.

1. Spin the spinner. Write the subtraction problem in the first column.

2. Write the larger number below the dot at the right end of the number line.

3. Look at the smaller number. Decide how many jumps to make by hundreds, tens, and ones, moving backward on the number line. (For example: 122 = 1 hundred, 2 tens, and 2 ones.) Write the difference below the number line after each jump.

4. Record the final difference.

5. Repeat steps 1 to 4. Be sure to get a different problem.

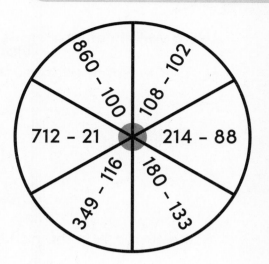

Example:	
141 − 122 =19	(number line: -1 -1 -10 -10 -100 ; 19 20 21 31 41 141)
	(blank number line)
	(blank number line)

🔍 **Investigate:** Write the equation shown on the number line.

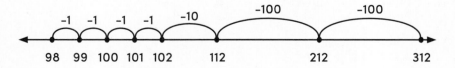

(number line: -1 -1 -1 -1 -10 -100 -100 ; 98 99 100 101 102 112 212 312)

✏️ **Write About It:** What is one of the most important ideas you learned from this lesson? Write about it on the back of the page.

#24 Name: _____

Use a variety of strategies to add within 1,000.

✓ **You will need:** base ten blocks

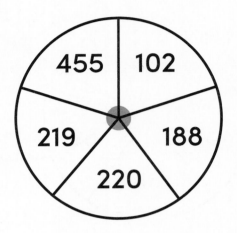
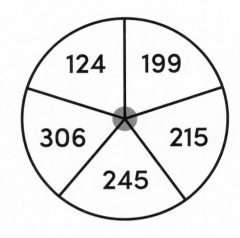

1. Spin both spinners. Write the numbers in a grid below.

2. Work with a partner. On your desk, use base ten blocks to model each addition problem. You may need to regroup.

3. Complete the problem in the grid.

4. Repeat steps 1 to 3. Be sure to get different numbers.

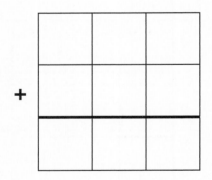
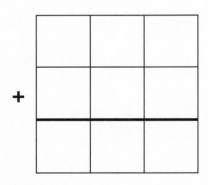
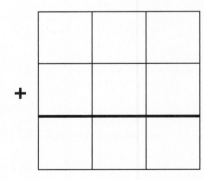

🔍 **Investigate:** Write your own three-digit addition problem with regrouping. Include the answer. For even more challenge, use only the digits 3, 4, 5, 6, 7, 8.

✏️ **Write About It:** On the back of the page, draw one of the base ten models you built. Did you find it helpful to use a model? Why or why not?

#25 Name: _____

Use a variety of strategies to subtract within 1,000.

✓ **You will need:** base ten blocks

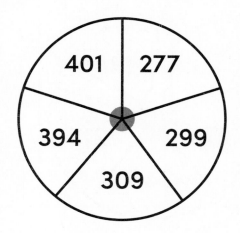
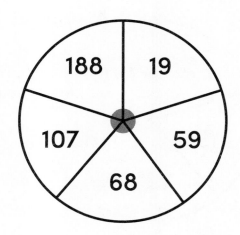

1. Spin both spinners. Write the numbers in a grid below. Place the larger number on top.

2. Work with a partner. On your desk, use base ten blocks to model the subtraction problem. You may need to regroup.

3. Compete the problem in the grid.

4. Repeat steps 1 to 3. Be sure to get different numbers.

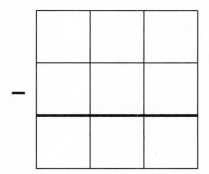
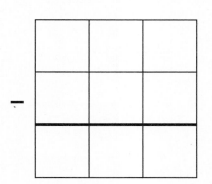
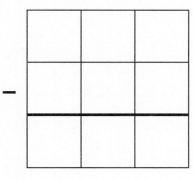

🔍 **Investigate:** Write your own three-digit subtraction problem with regrouping. Include the answer. For even more challenge, use only the digits 1, 2, 3, 4, 5, 6.

 Write About It: Can you tell that you will need to regroup just by looking at a subtraction problem? On the back of the page, write about how you know.

Multiply one-digit whole numbers by 10.

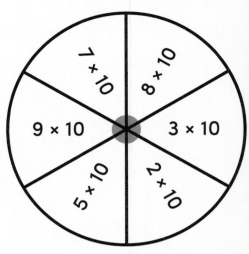

✓ **You will need:** base ten blocks

1. Spin the spinner. Write the multiplication problem below.

2. On your desk, model the multiplication problem using base ten blocks. Then, draw a picture next to the problem.

3. Find the product.

4. Repeat steps 1 to 3. Be sure to get a different problem.

Example: $4 \times 10 =$ __40__ 4 × 1 ten = 4 tens 4 tens = 40	

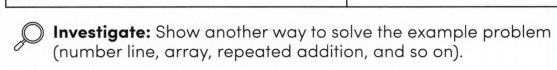

🔍 **Investigate:** Show another way to solve the example problem (number line, array, repeated addition, and so on).

✏️ **Write About It:** What is one question you had during this lesson? Did you find the answer? Write about it on the back of the page.

#27 Name: _____

Multiply one-digit whole numbers by multiples of 10.

✓ **You will need:** base ten blocks

1. Spin the spinner. Write the multiplication problem.

2. On your desk, model the multiplication problem using base ten blocks. Then, draw a picture next to the problem.

3. Find the product.

4. Repeat steps 1 to 3. Be sure to get a different problem.

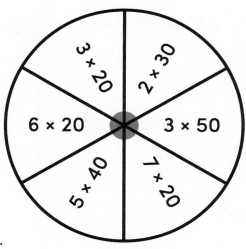

Example: $4 \times 20 = \underline{80}$ 4×2 tens = 8 tens 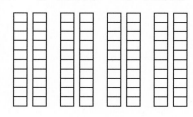 8 tens = 80	

🔍 **Investigate:** On the back of the page, show another way to solve the example problem (number line, array, repeated addition, and so on).

✏️ **Write About It:** On the back of the page, use the information from one of the multiplication problems to write a word problem.

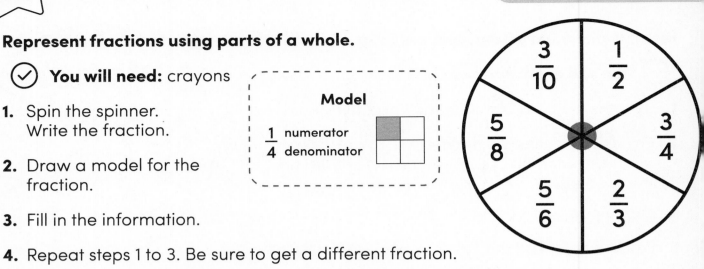

#28   Name: _____

Represent fractions using parts of a whole.

◯ **You will need:** crayons

1. Spin the spinner. Write the fraction.

2. Draw a model for the fraction.

3. Fill in the information.

4. Repeat steps 1 to 3. Be sure to get a different fraction.

Model

$\frac{1}{4}$ numerator denominator

Fraction	Model	Number of parts out of the whole	Number of equal parts of the whole
Example: $\frac{1}{4}$		1	4

🔍 **Investigate:** Look at each of your models. Are the equal parts the same shape in each model? Are the parts the same size in each model? Explain.

✏️ **Write About It:** On the back of the page, define the terms *numerator* and *denominator* in your own words.

★ **#29** **Name:** _____

Represent fractions using parts of a set.

✓ **You will need:** number cube • red, blue, and green counters • crayons

1. Roll the number cube to get the number of blue counters.

2. Roll the number cube to get the number of red counters.

3. Roll the number cube to get the number of green counters.

4. Place the counters on your desk and create a colorful worm.

5. Draw a picture of the worm you made. Use crayons to color.

6. How many counters do you have in all? _____

7. How many counters are blue? _____

   What fraction of the worm is blue? _____

8. How many counters are red? _____

   What fraction of the worm is red? _____

9. How many counters are green? _____

   What fraction of the worm is green? _____

🔍 **Investigate:** Draw eight stars. Shade some of the stars. What fraction of the set is shaded?

✏️ **Write About It:** On the back of the page, define the term *fraction* in your own words.

#30 Name: _____

Represent fractions on a number line.

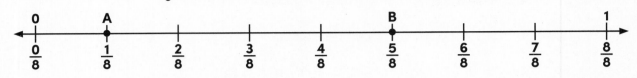

The number line below is divided into 8 equal parts. We can see that point A represents the distance from 0 to $\frac{1}{8}$. Point B represents the distance from 0 to $\frac{5}{8}$.

1. Pick a point on the number line below. Label it point X.

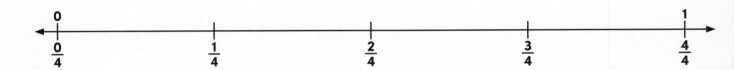

2. How far is point X from 0 on the number line? _____

3. How many equal lengths is the number line divided into? _____

4. What fraction represents one whole? _____

5. Pick three points on the number line below. Label them points A, B, and C.

6. How far is point C from 0 on the number line? _____

7. How many equal lengths is the number line divided into? _____

8. Which is farther from 0 on the number line: point A or point B? _____

9. What fraction represents one whole? _____

🔍 **Investigate:** On the back of the page, draw a number line. Divide it into three equal parts. Label: $\frac{0}{3}$, $\frac{1}{3}$, $\frac{2}{3}$, and $\frac{3}{3}$.

✏️ **Write About It:** Look at the example number line at the top of the page. What does the length between each mark on the number line represent? Explain.

Represent unit fractions on a number line.

✓ **You will need:** Fraction Bars (page 63) • scissors • glue • crayons

We can use fraction bars to represent and locate points on a number line. Here's how:

> A **unit fraction** is a fraction that has 1 as its numerator.

1. Choose a set of fraction bars. Cut them apart. Glue them in place on a number line below.

2. At the end of each fraction, place a mark on the number line. Then, write the fraction under each mark to show its distance from 0.

3. Color the fraction bar to show the distance between 0 and the unit fraction. Then, circle the unit fraction.

4. Repeat steps 1 to 3 with a different set of fraction bars.

Example:

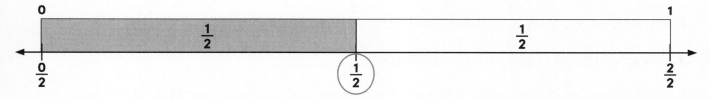

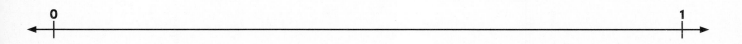

🔍 **Investigate:** Choose a fraction. Show two different ways to represent it (for example, fraction bars, number line, parts of a whole, parts of a set).

✏️ **Write About It:** In your own words, define the term *unit fraction*. Give some examples.

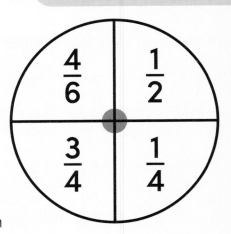

★ **#32** Name: _____

Use fraction bars to find equivalent fractions.

✓ **You will need:** Fraction Bars (page 63) • scissors • glue • crayons

1. Cut apart the fraction bars along the dotted lines.

2. Spin the spinner to get a fraction.

3. Glue the 1 whole fraction bar in place. Find a fraction bar that shows your fraction. Color part of the fraction bar to show the fraction. Glue it in place below the 1 whole fraction bar.

4. Look for another fraction that is equivalent, or covers the same space. Color part of the fraction bar to show the equivalent fraction. Glue it in place.

5. Write the equivalent fractions in the last column.

Example:	
	$\frac{1}{3} = \frac{2}{6}$

🔍 **Investigate:** Look at the fraction bars. Name three fractions that are equivalent to $\frac{1}{2}$.

✏️ **Write About It:** On the back of the page, define the term *equivalent fraction* in your own words.

#33 Name: _____

Use fraction bars to compare fractions.

✓ **You will need:** Fraction Bars (page 63) • scissors • glue • crayons

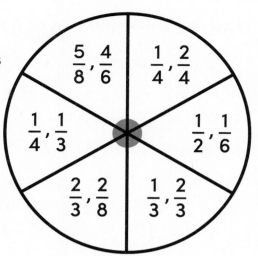

1. Cut apart the fraction bars along the dotted lines.

2. Spin the spinner to get fractions to compare.

3. Glue the 1 whole fraction bar in place. Choose fraction bars that show each fraction. Color the fraction bars to show the fractions. Glue them in place, one model under the other to compare.

4. Use the symbols <, =, or > to compare.

Example:

1			
$\frac{1}{4}$	$\frac{1}{4}$	$\frac{1}{4}$	$\frac{1}{4}$

| $\frac{1}{6}$ | $\frac{1}{6}$ | $\frac{1}{6}$ | $\frac{1}{6}$ | $\frac{1}{6}$ | $\frac{1}{6}$ |

$\frac{2}{4}$ ⊙ $\frac{2}{6}$

🔍 **Investigate:** Choose one fraction that is greater than $\frac{1}{2}$. Choose another fraction that is less than $\frac{1}{2}$. Cut out the fraction bars and color each fraction. Place the fraction bars in order, from least to greatest.

✏️ **Write About It:** On the back of the page, write about the steps you took to solve the problem.

#34 Name: _____

Express whole numbers as fractions.

✓ **You will need:** scissors • glue

1. Cut out the fraction models at the bottom of the page. Look carefully at the two example problems.

2. Spin the spinner. Record the fraction in the first column.

3. Find the fraction model that matches the fraction. Glue in place.

4. In the last column, write the fraction and the whole number.

5. Repeat steps 1 to 3. Be sure to get a different fraction.

Example: $\frac{5}{5}$	$\boxed{\frac{1}{5}\ \frac{1}{5}\ \frac{1}{5}\ \frac{1}{5}\ \frac{1}{5}}$	$\frac{5}{5}$ = 1
Example: $\frac{5}{1}$	▧ ▧ ▧ ▧ ▧	$\frac{5}{1}$ = 5

🔍 **Investigate:** Write two fractions that are both equal to 1. On the back of the page, draw a picture to show each fraction.

✏️ **Write About It:** On the back of the page, write about how the fractions $\frac{6}{6}$ and $\frac{6}{1}$ are the same and different.

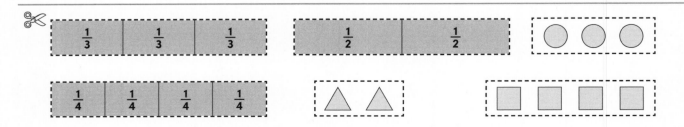

40

Learn about elapsed time.

⊘ **You will need:** two number cubes

1. Circle a wake-up time.   **7:00   7:05   7:08   7:10   7:12**

2. Find out how long each activity will take.
   Roll two number cubes and find the sum.

   Eat breakfast _____ minutes   **Brush teeth and comb hair** _____ minutes

   Get dressed _____ minutes   **Walk to the bus stop** _____ minutes

3. How much time elapsed between the wake-up time and arriving at the bus stop?
   Use the number line to find out.

   a. Mark the wake-up time.

   b. How much time does each activity take? Move forward that many units.

   c. Mark the arrival time at the bus stop.

   d. Find the elapsed time by counting the units between the two times.

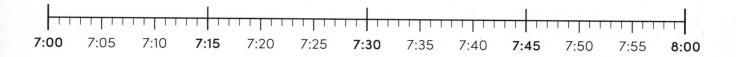

7:00   7:05   7:10   **7:15**   7:20   7:25   **7:30**   7:35   7:40   **7:45**   7:50   7:55   **8:00**

4. How much time elapsed between the wake-up time
   and the arrival at the bus stop?   _____ minutes

   🔍 **Investigate:** On a separate sheet of paper, redo the activity. This time use your
   own information. What time do you wake up? How long does it take you to eat
   breakfast, get dressed, and so on? Find the elapsed time between when you
   wake up and when you arrive at the bus stop or school.

   ✏️ **Write About It:** On the back of the page, define the term *elapsed time* in your
   own words.

#36 Name: _____

Learn about elapsed time.

Softball (3:30)   Recess (1:45)   Snack (10:00)

Cheerleading (3:20)   Book Club (2:15)   Morning Opening (8:05)

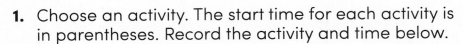

1. Choose an activity. The start time for each activity is in parentheses. Record the activity and time below.

2. Spin the spinner to find the elapsed time. Record below.

3. Use the number line below to help you find out when the activity ends.

4. Repeat steps 1 to 3. Be sure to get a different elapsed time.

Start Time	Elapsed Time	End Time
Art Class / 4:05	23 minutes	4:28

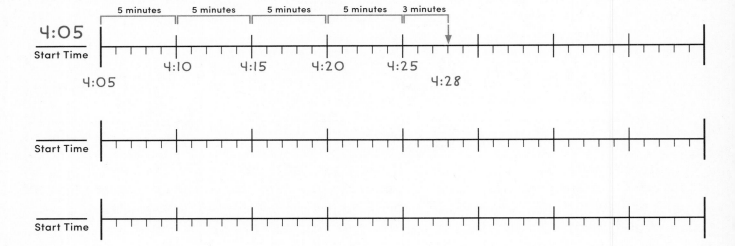

Investigate: Find out how much time you are in school every day. Describe the steps you took to find out.

Write About It: On the back of the page, write about how you solved one of the problems.

42

Learn about standard units of measure.

> A **gram (g)** is a metric unit for measuring mass (or weight). A paper clip is about 1 gram.
>
> A **kilogram (kg)** is a metric unit for measuring mass (or weight). A 1-liter bottle of water is about 1 kilogram. One kilogram equals 1,000 grams.

1. Think about objects in your classroom or at home. Write down three objects you think should be measured in grams. Write down three objects you think should be measured in kilograms.

Items Measured in Grams	Items Measured in Kilograms

> A **liter (L)** is a metric unit for measuring liquid volume. Some water bottles hold about 1 liter of liquid.

2. Think about containers at home and at school. Write down three containers that hold more than 1 liter of liquid. Write down three containers that hold less than 1 liter of liquid.

More Than One Liter	Less Than One Liter

 Investigate: What item in your classroom do you think weighs the most? What item in your classroom do you think weighs the least? Would you use grams or kilograms to measure each?

 Write About It: What is one of the questions you had during the lesson? Did you find the answer? Write your answer on the back of the page.

#38 Name: _____

Solve word problems involving mass and volume.

For each word problem, spin the spinner to fill in the missing numbers. Write an equation or draw a model. Then solve.

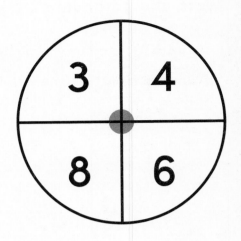

1. It takes 80 liters of water to fill up the bathtub.

    Pei poured _____ liters of water into the tub.

    How many more liters of water will Pei need?

2. Tina's mother bought _____ bottles of 2-liter soda for a birthday party. How many liters of soda will she have in all?

3. Rahsaan is packing a suitcase full of medical supplies to take on an airplane. The weight limit is 24 kilograms. Each package of medical supplies weighs _____ kilograms. How many packages can Rahsaan take in all?

4. Mr. Sanchez has a restaurant. He made _____ kilograms of meatballs on Monday, _____ kilograms of meatballs on Tuesday, and _____ kilograms of meatballs on Wednesday. How many kilograms of meatballs did Mr. Sanchez make in all?

🔍 **Investigate:** On the back of the page, write a word problem using mass or volume to show the sum of two quantities.

✏️ **Write About It:** Think about the terms *mass* and *volume*. On the back of the page, write about how the terms are the same and different.

Make a pictograph.

1. Spin the spinner to find out how many boxes of candy each student sold.

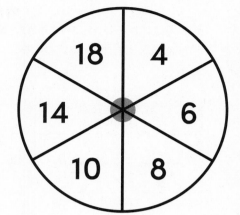

Tom sold _____ boxes of candy.

Juan sold _____ boxes of candy.

Tekia sold _____ boxes of candy.

Lily sold _____ boxes of candy.

2. Use the data to complete the picture graph.

Title: _____

Student	Boxes of Candy Sold										
Tom											
Juan											
Tekia											
Lily											

Key: = 2 boxes of candy

 Investigate: Write two questions that can be answered by looking at the information on the pictograph.

1. _____

2. _____

 Write About It: Write two statements about the pictograph.

1. _____

2. _____

Make a bar graph.

1. Ask students in your class to vote on their favorite pet. Use tally marks to keep track of their choices.

Pet	Tally Marks	Total
Cat		
Dog		
Bird		
Fish		
Hamster		

2. Create a bar graph showing the information.

Title: _____

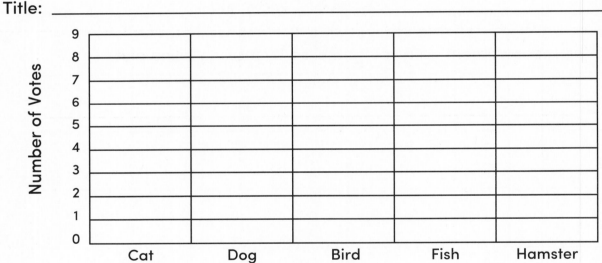

Investigate: Write two questions that can be answered by looking at the information on the bar graph.

1. _____

2. _____

Write About It: Write two statements about the bar graph.

1. _____

2. _____

Measure objects to the nearest $\frac{1}{4}$ inch and show the data on a line plot.

✓ **You will need:** inch ruler

1. Look around the classroom. Find five items that are less than 4 inches long.

2. List each object below. Measure each length to the nearest $\frac{1}{4}$ inch. Record.

Name of Object	Length

3. Record the measurement data you gathered by making a line plot.

Title: _____

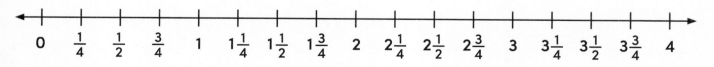

Measurements in Inches

🔍 **Investigate:** What is the difference between a bar graph and a line plot? When might you use each type?

✏️ **Write About It:** On the back of the page, write about the steps you took to make sure your measurements are accurate.

Measure objects to the nearest $\frac{1}{4}$ inch and show the data on a line plot.

✓ **You will need:** inch ruler

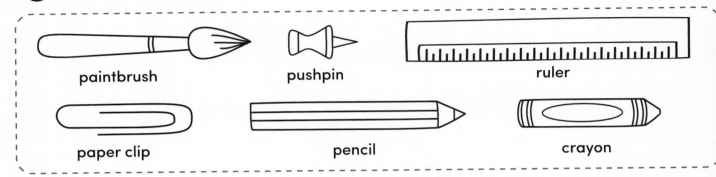

paintbrush   pushpin   ruler

paper clip   pencil   crayon

1. Choose four objects. Measure the length of each to the nearest $\frac{1}{4}$ inch. Record below.

Name of Object	Length

2. Record the measurement data by making a line plot.

Title: _____

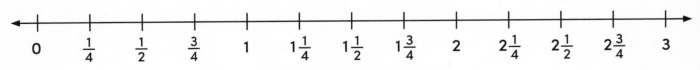

Measurements in Inches

🔍 **Investigate:** Look at the data you collected. Make one statement about the line plot.

✏️ **Write About It:** On the back of the page, write one question that can be answered by looking at the information shown on the line plot.

Learn about area measurement.

 You will need: geoboard • rubber bands • pencil

The **area** of a shape is the amount of space inside it.
A **unit square** has one square unit of area. We can
measure area by counting the number of square units.

1 unit [unit square] ← unit square
1 unit

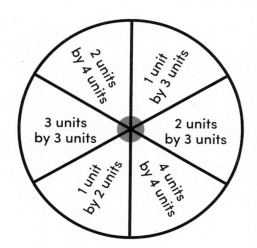

1. Model each figure on the geoboard. Find the area.

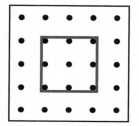

2 units by 2 units

_____ square units

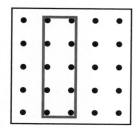

4 units by 1 unit

_____ square units

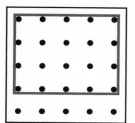

3 units by 4 units

_____ square units

2. Spin the spinner to find the dimensions of a figure. Model the figure
on the geoboard. Draw the figure below. Then, find the area. Repeat.

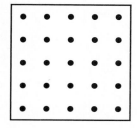

_____ square units

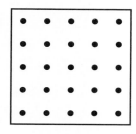

_____ square units

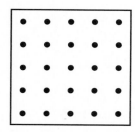

_____ square units

 Investigate: Use your geoboard to explore. Can you make two different
figures that have the same area? Draw them on the back of the page.

 Write About It: Look at these two figures.
Are they the same shape? Why or why not?
Write your answer on the back of the page.

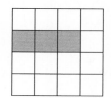 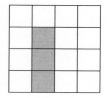

#44 Name: _____

Use unit squares to measure the area of quadrilaterals.

✓ **You will need:** scissors

1. Cut apart the unit squares at the bottom of the page.

2. Create a quadrilateral on your desk using four or more unit squares. Draw a picture below to show your work.

3. Find the area of each figure.

4. Repeat steps 2 and 3.

Create a quadrilateral.	Find the area of each figure.
	_____ square units
	_____ square units

🔍 **Investigate:** Imagine that you are telling someone how to create a unit square. What would you say?

✏️ **Write About It:** On the back of the page, write about how you determined the area of one of the quadrilaterals you created.

✂️

Find the area of squares and rectangles by counting unit squares.

✓ **You will need:** 1-inch tiles • crayons

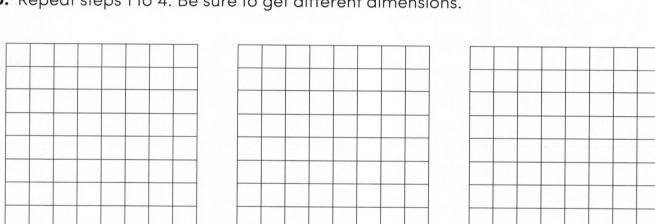

1. Spin the spinner to get the dimensions of a figure.

2. Build the figure on your desk using 1-inch tiles.

3. Show your work by coloring the squares on the grid.

4. Count the number of square inches to find the area. Record below.

5. Repeat steps 1 to 4. Be sure to get different dimensions.

_____ square inches   _____ square inches   _____ square inches

 Investigate: Can you build two figures that have different dimensions but the same area? Explain.

 Write About It: On the back of the page, write a definition of the term *area* in your own words.

#46 Name: _____

Find the area of irregular shapes by counting square units.

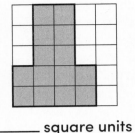 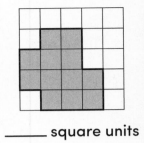

✓ **You will need:** crayons or markers

1. Find the area of each shape.

2. On the grid below, create a Zany Pet Critter out of six shapes. Make each shape a different color. Here's how:

   a. Create a blue shape with an area of 6 square units.

   b. Create two identical shapes that are each larger than the blue shape. Color one red and the other green.

   c. Create a yellow and an orange shape that each have an area of 4 square units.

   d. Create a pink shape with an area of your choice.

   e. Record the square area of each shape below.

3. Add eyes, ears, a mouth, and maybe even feet.

_____ square units   _____ square units

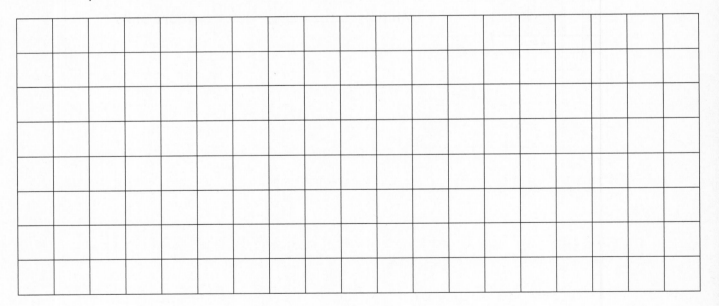

Red _____ square units   Blue _____ square units   Orange _____ square units

Green _____ square units   Yellow _____ square units   Pink _____ square units

🔍 **Investigate:** How did you determine the area of the red shape?

✏️ **Write About It:** On the back of the page, explain why the area of each figure is labeled "square units" instead of "units."

Name: _____

Use multiplication to find the area of figures.

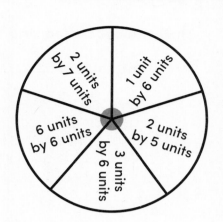

✓ **You will need:** crayons or markers

1. Spin the spinner to find the dimensions of a rectangle.

2. Create the rectangle on the grid. Color the squares to show the area.

3. Find the area of each rectangle.

4. Count the squares to make sure the area is correct.

5. Repeat steps 1 to 4. Be sure to get different dimensions.

Example:

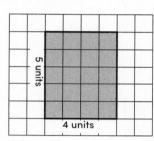

Count the units on one side. ___5___

Count the units on the bottom. ___4___

Multiply. ___5___ × ___4___ = ___20___ square units

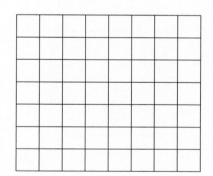

Count the units on one side. _____

Count the units on the bottom. _____

Multiply. _____ × _____ = _____ square units

Count the units on one side. _____

Count the units on the bottom. _____

Multiply. _____ × _____ = _____ square units

 Investigate: How many figures can you create that each have an area of 20 square inches? Draw pictures on graph paper to help.

Write About It: On the back of the page, write about how you solved one of the problems.

#48 Name: _____

Use multiplication and addition to find the area of special figures.

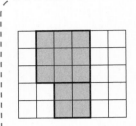

1. Find the area of individual sections.
   3 × 3 = 9 square units
   2 × 2 = 4 square units

2. Then add.
   9 + 4 = 13 square units

The area of the figure is 13 square units.

Find the area of each figure.

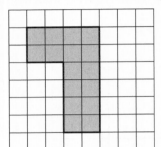

Area of section: _____ sq units

Area of section: _____ sq units

Total area: _____ + _____ = _____ sq units

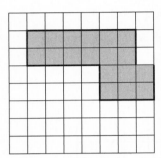

Area of section: _____ sq units

Area of section: _____ sq units

Total area: _____ + _____ = _____ sq units

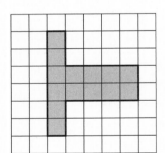

Area of section: _____ sq units

Area of section: _____ sq units

Total area: _____ + _____ = _____ sq units

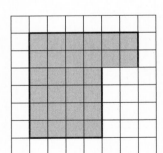

Area of section: _____ sq units

Area of section: _____ sq units

Total area: _____ + _____ = _____ sq units

 Investigate: Is there more than one way to separate this figure into rectangles to find its area? Use the back of the page to explain your answer.

 Write About It: Did you learn anything new about how to find the area of a figure in this lesson? Write your answer on the back of the page.

Find the perimeter of polygons.

The distance around a polygon is the **perimeter**.
To find the perimeter, add the length of the sides.

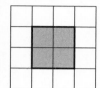

Each side is 2 units long.
The perimeter is 8 units.
2 + 2 + 2 + 2 = 8 units.

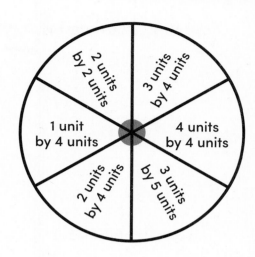

2 units by 2 units
3 units by 4 units
1 unit by 4 units
4 units by 4 units
2 units by 4 units
3 units by 5 units

1. Spin the spinner to find the dimensions of each polygon. Draw the outline of each figure on the grid. Find the perimeter. Record.

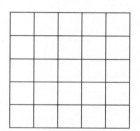

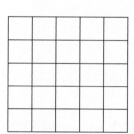

_____ + _____ + _____ + _____ = _____ units   _____ + _____ + _____ + _____ = _____ units

2. Levi wants to buy fencing to put around his garden. Two sides of the garden are 8 feet. The other two sides are twice as long. How much fencing should Levi buy?

Draw a picture to show the problem.

Write an equation. _____

 Investigate: Draw two rectangles that have the same perimeter but are different shapes.

 Write About It: On the back of the page, write how you solved the word problem.

#50 Name: _____

Find the perimeter and area of polygons.

✓ **You will need:** geoboard • crayons

1. Model each figure on the geoboard.
Find the perimeter and area.

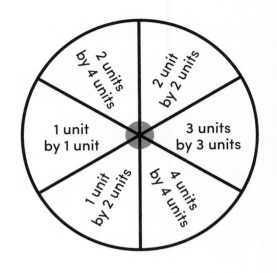

3 units by 2 units

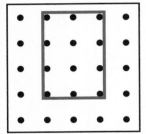

Perimeter: _____ units

Area: _____ sq units

4 units by 3 units

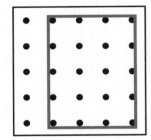

Perimeter: _____ units

Area: _____ sq units

2. Spin the spinner to find the dimensions of a figure. Model the figure on the geoboard. Draw the figure below. Then, find the perimeter and area. Repeat.

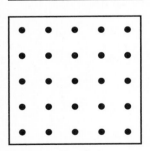

Perimeter: _____ units

Area: _____ sq units

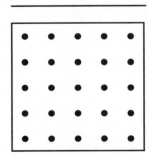

Perimeter: _____ units

Area: _____ sq units

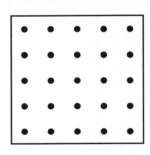

Perimeter: _____ units

Area: _____ sq units

 Investigate: On the geoboard, create two rectangles that have the same area but different perimeters. Draw a sketch to show your work.

 Write About It: On the back of the page, describe when you could use what you know about perimeter and area to solve real-life problems.

#51 Name: _____

Learn about quadrilaterals.

A **quadrilateral** is a closed figure with four sides. There are different types of quadrilaterals, based on their sides and angles.

1. Draw examples of a rectangle.	**2.** Draw examples of a rhombus.
What attributes does a rectangle have?	What attributes does a rhombus have?
3. Draw examples of a trapezoid.	**4.** Draw examples of a square.
What attributes does a trapezoid have?	What attributes does a square have?

Investigate: Explain why a square can also be a rectangle and a rhombus.

Write About It: On the back of the page, define the term *closed figure* in your own words.

Note: You may want to use the Quadrilaterals guide on page 64 for reference.

#52 Name: _____

Learn about quadrilaterals.

1. Draw a square. Then draw a quadrilateral that is <u>not</u> a square.

Why is the quadrilateral not a square?

2. Draw a rhombus. Then draw a quadrilateral that is <u>not</u> a rhombus.

Why is the quadrilateral not a rhombus?

3. Draw a rectangle. Then draw a quadrilateral that is <u>not</u> a rectangle.

Why is the quadrilateral not a rectangle?

4. Draw a trapezoid. Then draw a quadrilateral that is <u>not</u> a trapezoid.

Why is the quadrilateral not a trapezoid?

Investigate: Lee says that all rectangles are quadrilaterals and all quadrilaterals are rectangles. Is he right? Explain.

Write About It: What is one question you had during this lesson? Did you find the answer? Write your answer on the back of the page.

Note: You may want to use the Quadrilaterals guide on page 64 for reference.

#53 **Name:** _____

Partition shapes into equal parts.

Here is one way to partition the square into equal parts. One part is $\frac{1}{3}$.	Show another way to partition the square into equal parts. Label one part.
Show one way to partition the circle into equal parts. Label one part.	Show another way to partition the circle into equal parts. Label one part.
Show one way to partition the rectangle into equal parts. Label one part. 	Show another way to partition the rectangle into equal parts. Label one part. 

 Investigate: Is this circle divided into four equal parts? Explain.

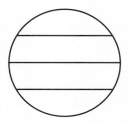

 Write About It: On the back of the page, define the term *partition* in your own words.

Create a polygon given one fractional part.

1. Look at the fractional part of the figure. Complete the polygon.

This shape is $\frac{1}{3}$ of a rectangle.

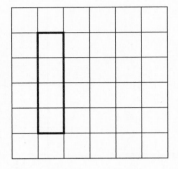

This shape is $\frac{1}{2}$ of a hexagon.

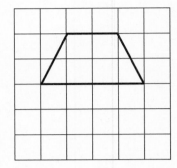

This shape is $\frac{1}{4}$ of a square.

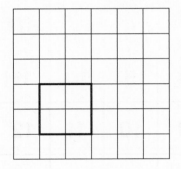

This shape is $\frac{1}{2}$ of a rectangle.

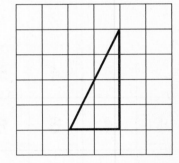

2. It's your turn. Draw a fractional part of a figure. Then fill in the blanks.

This shape is

_____

of a

_____ .

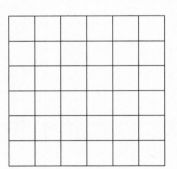

This shape is

_____

of a

_____ .

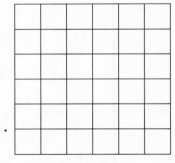

 Investigate: Try an extra challenge!
This shape is $\frac{1}{2}$ of a rhombus.
Complete the polygon.

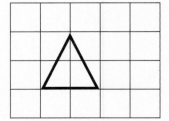

Write About It: On the back of the page,
write about how you solved one of the problems.

Addition Table

Look at the Addition Table. Notice that there are rows and columns.
The rows go across. The columns go up and down.

COLUMN

ROW

+	0	1	2	3	4	5	6	7	8	9	10
0	0	1	2	3	4	5	6	7	8	9	10
1	1	2	3	4	5	6	7	8	9	10	11
2	2	3	4	5	6	7	8	9	10	11	12
3	3	4	5	6	7	8	9	10	11	12	13
4	4	5	6	7	8	9	10	11	12	13	14
5	5	6	7	8	9	10	11	12	13	14	15
6	6	7	8	9	10	11	12	13	14	15	16
7	7	8	9	10	11	12	13	14	15	16	17
8	8	9	10	11	12	13	14	15	16	17	18
9	9	10	11	12	13	14	15	16	17	18	19
10	10	11	12	13	14	15	16	17	18	19	20

Multiplication Table

Look at the Multiplication Table. Notice that there are rows and columns. The rows go across. The columns go up and down.

COLUMN ↓

ROW →

x	0	1	2	3	4	5	6	7	8	9	10
0	0	0	0	0	0	0	0	0	0	0	0
1	0	1	2	3	4	5	6	7	8	9	10
2	0	2	4	6	8	10	12	14	16	18	20
3	0	3	6	9	12	15	18	21	24	27	30
4	0	4	8	12	16	20	24	28	32	36	40
5	0	5	10	15	20	25	30	35	40	45	50
6	0	6	12	18	24	30	36	42	48	54	60
7	0	7	14	21	28	35	42	49	56	63	70
8	0	8	16	24	32	40	48	56	64	72	80
9	0	9	18	27	36	45	54	63	72	81	90
10	0	10	20	30	40	50	60	70	80	90	100

Fraction Bars

For Activity #31 (page 37)

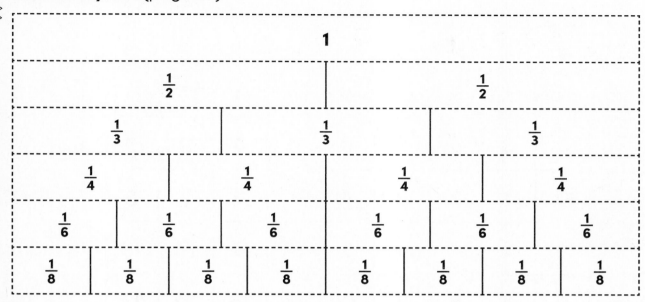

For Activities #32 and #33 (pages 38–39)

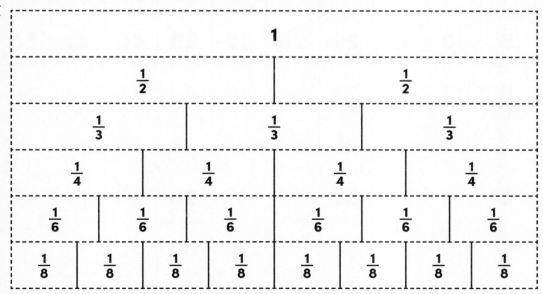

Quadrilaterals

Quadrilaterals are two-dimensional closed figures. They have four straight sides. Quadrilaterals are named by their sides and angles.

Rectangle

- 2 pairs of opposite sides are parallel
- 2 pairs of sides are equal lengths
- 4 right angles

Rhombus

- 2 pairs of opposite sides are parallel
- 4 sides are equal lengths

Square

- 2 pairs of opposite sides are parallel
- 4 sides are equal lengths
- 4 right angles

Trapezoid

- At least one set of parallel sides

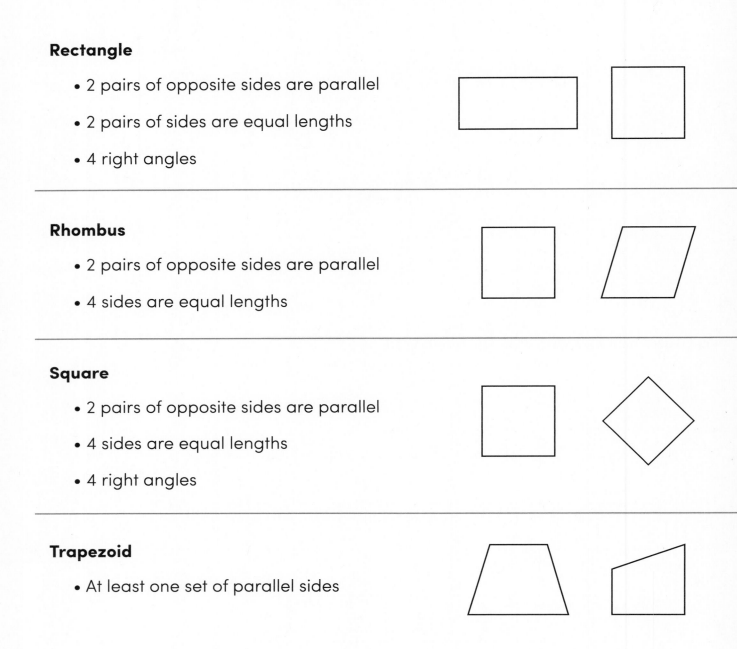

You may want to use this information as a resource guide for activities 51, 52, 53, and 54.